A Northern Calendar

Ira Sadoff

A NORTHERN
CALENDAR.

DAVID R. GODINE · BOSTON

A Godine Poetry Chapbook
Fourth Series

First published in 1982 by
DAVID R. GODINE, PUBLISHER, INC.
306 Dartmouth Street
Boston, Massachusetts 02116

Library of Congress Cataloging in Publication Data

Sadoff, Ira.
    A northern calendar.
    (A Godine poetry chapbook; 4th ser.)
    I. Title.
PS3569.A26N6   811'.54   80-83949
ISBN 0-87923-367-2

Some of the poems in this book first appeared in the follow-
ing publications: *The American Poetry Review, Antaeus, Crazy
Horse, The Missouri Review, The New Republic, The Paris Re-
view, The Partisan Review, Ploughshares, Unicorn Books Poetry
Pamphlet Series, Virginia Quarterly Review.* "January: First
Light" first appeared in *The New Yorker,* copyright © 1980,
The New Yorker Magazine, Inc. "Bleak House," "My Wife's
Upstairs," and "The Subject Matter" first appeared in *Poetry.*

Printed in the United States of America

PS
3569
A26
N6
1982

To Dianne again,
To Peter & Natalie
John & Mickey
and my other friends in Maine

Contents

January: First Light

It's the path
of the old railroad tracks,
just before light. No noise:
the barn owl drifting into sleep,
the birds not yet awake.
The iron scars
have been melted down
for a war long fought and gone.
Then the evening edged out
by the first band of light,
across the strips of trees.
I know
I don't have long to go:
the sleepless night that brought me
to the woods behind the house
is over now, and what fears I had
I left behind me there.
In the distance I make out rabbit tracks
and behind them, something larger,
a dog perhaps, on its trail.
The trail leads nowhere
and the rabbit's safe.
A world without predators: the parent's
dream. Why won't it pass?
Look: the starling's pulled that ribbon
of worm, the day's unraveling,
we're moving on, exhausted, ready to begin.

February: Pemaquid Point

The lighthouse as an image
of loneliness has its limits.

For as we stand on the shore
of this ocean, the crusted snow

on the hills and grass
dispersed beneath it, that tower

seems a place where people gather
some vision of themselves: the marriage

of rock to water, of wave to snail
washed up on shore. We're small,

and waving to the lobster boat—
which could be miles away or close

enough to raise our voices to—makes
us wish our journeys took us further,

past witness, to a scene
where we belonged. A man in blue

pulls up his net, tiny fish
swim free from it. And the man

pulling anchor, whose strength
pulls him further from the shore,

pays tribute to our rootlessness.
As he shouts to start the engine up,

to take his course, he leaves us
in the distance, the repeated ritual

of his wake. And like the water
stirred against the lighthouse wall,

breaking up, wave after wave, we
forget ourselves. Learn our place.

On First Sighting a Man

The widows seem curious, as do the young.
The ships have come, full of them, these men
with flat, symmetrical frames. How bored
the married women are with them, no one can say.
Wash hangs on the line, white flags
not of surrender or peace: they signal
something more. Do they miss their men?

Can you miss a place you've never been?
I remember waking once, the sharp chill
of Stockholm stinging from my sleep, harbors
crowded with so many ships the water seemed
precarious, superfluous. I was waving goodbye
to my mother and thought only of my setting
at the table. My meal. How I wanted it saved.

I've never been to Sweden, but wish I had.
In the same way, or in a different way,
these women will embrace men at their stations;
I wonder when they hold their frigid limbs—
which threaten crumbling at the touch—do these
men stand up to their imaginings? The washboard,
the stiff sheets hung out that won't dry in snow,

that stay cold when you sleep on them, if they
resemble the shape of men they've lost,
who'd want them back? I can't guess
the logic of it, but I can love the harbor in a storm,
the way loose planks fly up from the wharf
and strike the anchored ships. I know what harm
    they do.
I've never been to sea. But I could learn to care for it.

Early April Morning: Fairfield, Maine

In our house it's still dark,
the shapes of furniture indistinct,
but my attention drifts out the window,
I'm vaguely happy keeping vigil at the stove.

One moment the sun is shining,
the next a wet snow saturates the hills.
Dark clouds set the pack of dogs barking,
the cows start their slow ride to the barn.

Every morning, the same quick change.
I'm daydreaming of the boy shoveling manure
from the steaming barn, and my wife appears
half-dazed in her robe, rubbing sleep from her eyes.

She's been dreaming of the future: we're
living in two different countries, and in between
there's a letter lost on the surface
of the ocean. Who knows what it contains?

While we wonder what this means, the boy's
been driven off to school, the chained-up
dogs whine in his absence, and the snow's left
such a small impression: a slick, wet road.

Poem Beginning with a Quotation from My Mother

Life is short, enough.
Yesterday it threatened rain
all day. Clouds dropped down
and darkened, but never fell.

The wells deserved it, dry.
Instead the green leaves redden
and drop. Milkweed scatters
its small feathers on the lawn.

Today I walk the land
my father never owned.
Traveling far, I feel at home.
And there are so many names

of trees I've yet to learn:
alder, cedar, tulip, beech.
As one who's never satisfied,
who finds cruelty in pleasure,

I've walked these trails to powder,
lingered in this place too long.
My family history: in reverie
they walked the Russian plains,

sought salvation from the czar.
Where are they now? Distant enough
from one another they fear taps
on the shoulder, the telephone.

The way when I walk through a thicket
and surprise the thrush,
it flies away beyond my grasp.
I could have held it in my hand.

Now the sun is out, it shines.
In this light I pick up a leaf
that from a distance looked just like
a butterfly. I don't know what kind.

Sunrise: Two Artichokes and an Onion

This is for those who flower
to bitterness. For the flowers of abundance,
of too many petals: the green thorn-flower,
the flower scraped clean, whose buttery
heart must be eaten through.
                                    And its cousin
of so many layers, so often circled,
cast off, misunderstood. So it opens to emptiness:
those who know loss know that gesture
of giving, the pause between darkness
and first half-penny of sun.

It's morning now: the checkered clouds
rise over the hillside, blue and white
fields too distant, like a wish, to be touched.
To be consumed, to disappear, this is the desire
of those unloved, the red and green, the first light
we shy away from, those we want to flower for.

Walking Down Castro Street:
after Frank O'Hara

The streets of San Francisco
go on too long
which is a pleasant thing
like 'going out of our way'
when we're just out walking
without a destination in mind

I'm in one of those moods
when I'm ready for anything
walking without purpose or compulsion
which doesn't mean you're not compelling
but I'm paying attention to the arguments
in the gay bars and fresh pasta stores
and Japanese Germans with cameras and musicians
whistling Fats Waller on the street corners

Who knows where all this will lead to
is it the movie where Frank O'Hara appears
as a figure in a Larry Rivers painting
just because he might have observed these details
so casually they would all come together
in a loving assessment of the avenue
and the couples who love and hate one another
some of whom seem lost without French Roast coffee
and others who don't quite know where they're going
in no particular hurry to arrive

Summer Solstice:
In Praise of the Bourgeois

for Greg and Trisha

A few humbling things.
Outside my real house
there's an actual picket fence,
a flowerbox, one shady maple,
and a lawn too big to mow.
I said I'd never come to this.

I said a lot of things.
And sulked, tempestuous, as seasons
passed, unworthy of fierce attention.
My greatest fear: fathers grew fat
and dull, swayed and fell, weighed down
by small concessions to the ordinary.

So today's a kind of turning point.
First the days grew long,
now I can't keep up. So I'm left
with evenings, less of them, and a little light.

Tonight's excitement? A walk around
the block, counting inchworms dangling
from the trees. Watching neighbors clear dishes,
someone's grandpa tinker in his garage.
I wish I had a daughter to show them to.

This morning in the glare of sun
that shaped my vision of the road,
I sped past a hitchhiker, his life
possessions light enough to lie beside him
in a ditch. His sad face told a story I knew
too well. That's why I left him there.

And praised this day for standing still.

The Vacation in Miami: July, 1954

In his yellow swimsuit, in the heat of July,
they sent him to his room, the suggestion

of his father's hand. It was the shape
of a passing cloud—the burnished palm

left a taste in his mouth: charcoal.
A moment not worth remembering.

But the hotel and its ammonia smell, palm
trees bristling, seemed an invitation

to the ocean. He watched couples approach
the water cautiously, and grown-ups

protected by umbrellas from the acid heat.
The room, the white stucco walls, cut him off

from his small friends, the way a rubber band
breaks the circulation on a wrist. Blue.

The children whispered to each other
his punishment. He knew what they thought.

What was his crime? He could not quite remember it.
It had something to do with swimming out too far,

with firecrackers that fell from his pocket
while wrestling his father on the grass.

Exile seems too strong a word, and reminds him
of his father smoking cigarettes, waving

to strange women in their bathing suits,
following one to her room. But left alone

the boy swam out, caught his father's guilty slap.
And watched the Fourth of July from his window,

the darkened ocean reflecting evening sky,
his parents' argument, the fireworks' bright display.

Ashcroft, Colorado: July, 1979

So little continuance.

This ghost town is dead. Full
of photos we take back to our houses,
seven saloons, the shell of an old hotel,
a single outhouse and a memory
of miners buried where veins of silver

once were mined and traced. No ore
left to feed on: just that blue
expanse of sky and mountain peaks
where snow falls this and each July.

A child asked: 'Where
did all the cowboys go?'
and no one knows. We just imagine
a haze of rouge, hats, tall
boots and bar-slurred speech,

the stubble field on which we rest.
Just the blue phlox, jimson weed,
thin stalks leaning toward the light.
The earth drained of all its riches.

The same river forces its different waters
full, downstream. Now the sun's
too hot, too soon we'll freeze
when it drops from sight. Nothing to pan
or to pan out. No drama here. One moment

you're just gone, the next you're a stranger's
nostalgia, the decimated language: tense, past.

Entry

Today I did nothing.
I got up, ran a few miles,
took note of the dead squirrels
and leaves on the birches
turning disgracefully yellow
in August. Then I sat on my hands,
rested my exhausted body,
watched the weeds through the window.

I'm not proud of this,
I'm not proud of anything.
Like the man who bought too much
at the market, I want to take
everything back. The hours
without solitude, the moments of kindness,
come to so much change in the pockets.

It's a cold summer night: more stars
than sky. I can think clearly tonight.
I light a cigarette and sit back
in my chair, wondering where
is there left to advance?
I run my hand through my hair
and watch the circular moon
pull itself out of the earth.
Just like yesterday, and the day before,
only it pales in its diminishment,
the apple devoured a sliver at a time.

Family Reunion at China Lake

A mild breeze off the water: we watch
our fathers sail with the wind, travel
where they're taken, the carved-out shells
tilting leeward, tipped as if to fall.

While on the dock, a minor miracle:
a dragonfly sheds its reptile skin, tests
its wings, flies off and disappears.
Our bodies, free of such ambition,
seem substantial weight in summer's heat.
We won't repeat our small mistakes.

I know we've been here before,
wanting to bury our young bodies
in this icy lake. Frighten our parents
with disappearance, then rise up
minutes later in a dead man's float.
We wanted, for a moment, their hearts

to fail. Such a perfect risk! Fear
without danger, a gesture so unlike
what we've become. Now our children,
though they don't exist, might well
swim out beyond our sight.

The sun is out but the water's cold,
and though my cousins call, I won't go in.
The dragonfly buzzes and circles us,
looking so dangerous he does no harm.
In my hand I hold its rubber shell, the animal
past a useless vestige chewed away.

My Wife's Upstairs

My wife's upstairs,
hard at work.
I don't understand
what she thinks about
in that tiny room
looking out at the apple trees,
an ordinary field, a thread of stream.
She's thinking of something else.

It's a dreary day, though the foliage
makes its first appearance
on the locust trees, bales of hay
stacked neatly by the farmer's barn.
She's thinking of something else.
Surrounded by books, strands of hair
I imagine in her eyes, a gaze
she offers the window, a distance all her own.

Those books are long journeys,
train rides through the Urals,
parlors in which lovers meet
but can't openly speak. In the next room,
parents, the police, a nosy concierge.
Several kinds of intrigue.
She's so quiet as to be invisible.

I put my ear to the door,
every sense alert. So close
I can almost feel her pulse and breath.
But my wife's far away in that room,
out of the ordinary, fills that space
with longing, the aroma of fallen apples,
the space a single room can't hold.

The Subject Matter

How elusive—what we want
to speak of: a face
reflected in water, the buzz
of a bee from flower to flower.
Or was it mother
weeping by the campsite at all
the family outings? The drift of incidents
builds and builds, like the fire
that makes so many shapes and shadows
we don't know what to make of them. Yet
there were moments we seemed to cohere
to one another, to huddle close or hug
after long absences ....
                  The season
for memory is brief and clouded over,
but it strikes you that the sun was out,
you took the family photograph and the family
soon dispersed. Later on, the images
and details seemed too real, an explanation
of the hillside—but you can't find
yourself in the picture, and the flowers
growing over the meadow now are not the ones
we wanted to preserve, the ones we meant to pick.

Street Scene by Hopper

You think of yourself as a child
approaching this forgotten painting:
the drained color of the porch,
the light that strikes a figure
going out. And in the corner
of the canvas, you were afraid
something was buried in the shade
of the forsythia: cuff links, a brown
suitcase, your father's voice.

Mother will not dress herself, will not
come out. Then who's honking the horn?
What does it remind you of? The neighbors
crowding in the windows, afraid
to make a sound. They don't know
what they're entitled to—not the symmetry
of manners, not the drone of argument,
the muted flowers in a row. But you had the air
of confidence, the single pose
which got you through. That let you walk
past those windows, the dim
faces behind you now, those windows
breaking through their shapeless frames.

Bleak House

Drunks in the courtyard, dung and driftwood
floating down the Thames, and some
poor swine sweats over his accounts.
The error's his. Standing on the bridge
in lamplight, the stars barricaded
by a wall of clouds, he knows
what chance he has. And the do-gooder
who pulls him down is also without a penny,
doomed to room in a pauper's grave.

Reader, this body's a shapeless mass,
made to fall apart. You don't want to hear
about the boy with so much promise,
who marries to improve himself. The old grouch
who gives away all his money
with a smile. Dear reader, the happy ending's
this: a little girl in curls
marries, gives herself up, is kept
to death and doesn't get a single kiss.
So wipe off that smirk. Your rich uncle's coming
to dinner, he's left you his precious disease

Intimacy at First Light:
Bath, Maine, Shipyard

I.

Not to speak when we're so close
is to be small and shapeless, unlike the other,
small and not part of the clouds, the islands
of sky, the inhaled breath. To forget women
while gazing at their form. As when

the navies are formless, ships without number,
planted in the ocean as on plateaus or vales.
But peace in the countryside is speechless
and without form: the way you can't count sheep
in that meadow, the way footsteps disappear

on frozen ground. At the beginning of daylight,
the last flaking star, the flaking star
of evening, falls and grows dark in the hills
without shadow, falls without will, loses
its impulse, its crystal shape.

II.

The knowledge of her was like knowing
each day, familiar and therefore unknown.
She was without figure and a presence
that drew his attention: to think of her
was to create her form over and over again.

24

III.

The dull film of being, which we cannot see
or take in yet understand; the fission
of daylight, the colorless flesh which takes shape
in every mooning over someone else, in everyone
we wish to bring close by act or speech,

there lies the delight, the coldest spring
uncentered as it wanders into oceans,
the unreal anchor that makes ships seem
so still. So even without a word or breeze
we may move close and hold the bulk

of us as we pass from birth to death,
and take hold of what tatters and falls,
the tiny flag on the ship's mast, the signal
that stands without decoding, our shapes
as they remember us, the dismantling clouds.

Please

don't let the suckling pig be born.

I hate the way he roots his snout
through trash, finds exactly what he wants.

How he squeals and squirms upside down,
on the hook, waiting for the knife to come.

I don't want to satirize the civilized:
I remember uncle Harry snorting

rum from Sohio cans, elbowed up
in grease at his boss's small garage.

I could hear him curse, then be contrite,
lick his boots, slide his dolly back

beneath the broken Ford. The night they fired him
Harry's wife served up roast pig. Here they come,

the trail of pink and bloodied faces rising
from the womb—how they raise their snouts to suck,

how they're buried at their mother's breasts
safely out of view. They were Harry's pigs

but I can't blame him. I won't forget the blur
of grease sticking to our lips. We all dug in.

It's the shit they made us eat.

Villains

after Ritsos

We hate them all, though we're also proud of them.
Gradually we'll remember some, or build monuments
to those who brought them down. What better sign
of our concern? *Thank God they understood us,*
they knew everything before the fact.
A few are pulled by horses
tied to their ankles, sell brand-new clothes
at auctions, carry calling cards and deeds
to useless properties.
Mornings they'll disperse
from their basements, deep in conversation, refuse
a smoke—it's bad for their health. One on the subway,
knife in his raincoat, two in the Pentagon
peering down the throats of their missles; the oldest
on the ceiling, a nasty old man, ties his mother in knots
to the chandelier. Soon, in the upstairs apartment
we'll see the shades pulled up, the lights go on,
and the uninvited—those of us without distinction
or title, the sightseers—will knock to be let in
on a game of five-card stud. We know the deck is
        stacked
against us: we want to watch the way the cards are
        marked.

My Old German Girl Friend's

apartment was full of ties.
I lied to her every chance I got: straightened
my curly hair, learned manners to excess.
I would have sold my family's jewels
to share a single moment in her bed.

Past York Avenue, the rows of delicatessens,
past the East River basin where bodies
often floated up in plastic bags,
past the Willis Avenue Bridge, the free
trips to the South Bronx, I thought heaven

was bedding down in Hamburg, I thought
of taking photographs of every segment of her flesh
I feared I wouldn't remember, but I remember
every strained and unspoken moment
of adolescence: the day Kennedy was shot

I pumped that angry loss into Christa's small
center—shaky as I was, when the Berlin Wall
shot up out of nowhere, when my Russian grandma
intercepted our phone calls, heard the hard
syllables offer the obscenity of unguarded love,

I shivered some but would not stop.

The Invasion of the Body Snatchers

This fog over the body and mind,
this sleeping too long on the grill
of the mattress while morning pours in ....

It's ten below. The sun is shining
but it's too cold to go out. The children, true,
are bundled up, drive their snowmobiles
over the ice with a swishing sound, a sigh.

In the movies we could say
What's there to awaken for? and mean
the day's too long to gather in.

The lone squirrel on the roof,
looking at the last shell of pinecone,
the annoying noise of my wrist watch,
a reminder of how little gets done.

Last night in the dark we saw
a whole city taken over
by bodies without feeling, substitutes
for ourselves. The stone faces

of strangers in motion, without motive,
was somehow comic, as if
only a single face held close
could take us in, could threaten us.

Sleep takes us where we want. The woman
who paid me no attention suddenly appears,
sits on my lap and speaks, the red
smear of her lips the blur of desire.

Whereas, awake, the vision of the child,
obscured by the treeline it weaves through,
will not tempt: our gaze into innocence
is like the wind which chills them,

drags our bodies through the repetitions
we become, and like the spark
of daylight presses down on us.

Dersu Uzala

after Kurosawa

Morning. The plane rises,
tilts from side to side. My insides
a little raw, for no reason.

In the theater, the strained
images of Kurosawa come back
to me unchanged: sunrise in the taiga,
swamp grass bending, the long journey

of those who can't adapt: we touched,
secretly, as if ashamed by lust. We had our lives,
those we belonged to, and would not
give them up. To disappear and be far

from others isn't what we desire, it's
our escape. Sleeping by myself is barbarous,
so is sleeping with someone else.

Now, the tiny houses almost breathing,
the unmarked roads, snow blowing past
their borders, free and hardly visible ...

What is it I ask from you,
from anyone? The connection between strangers
is easy if intimate, barren
as a land explored but never farmed.

A tiger appeared in that forest,
so beautiful a savage it seemed
almost tame. But we grew closer
to its hunger, were taken back

by our fears. I don't want to go home,
and I can't stand a single place.
Your touch will be remembered, the wish
for friendship, which, in flight

might take us home but will not hold.